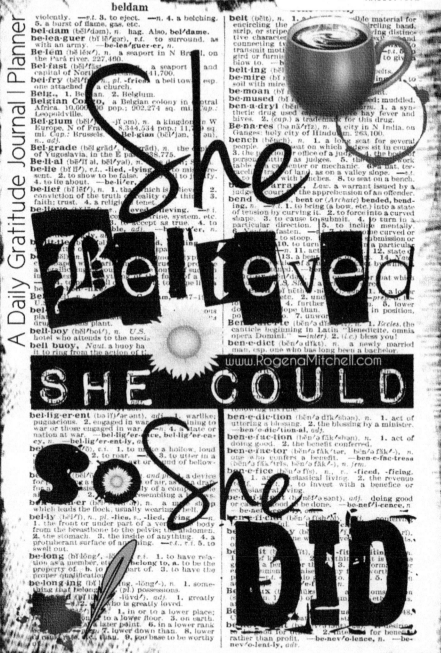

A Daily Gratitude Journal | Planner

ROGENA MITCHELL-JONES MANUSCRIPT SERVICE

ROGENA MITCHELL-JONES MANUSCRIPT SERVICE
ROGENA MITCHELL-JONES JOURNALS
WWW.ROGENAMITCHELL.COM

"She BELIEVED! And so should you. Always believe in yourself. You can do anything you put your mind to—so do it!

~ Rogena Mitchell

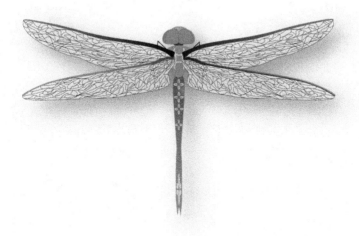

She believed she could so she did.

MONDAY

_____

_____

_____

_____

_____

TUESDAY

_____

_____

_____

_____

_____

WEDNESDAY

_____

_____

_____

_____

_____

THURSDAY

_____

_____

_____

_____

She believed she could so she did.

FRIDAY

SATURDAY

SUNDAY

"**Kindness** is the language which the deaf can hear
and the blind can see." ~ **Mark Twain**

She believed she could so she did.

MONDAY

TUESDAY

WEDNESDAY

THURSDAY

She believed she could so she did.

FRIDAY

SATURDAY

SUNDAY

"A lady's imagination is very rapid; it jumps from
admiration to love, from love to matrimony in a moment."
~ Jane Austen

She believed she could so she did.

MONDAY

TUESDAY

WEDNESDAY

THURSDAY

She believed she could so she did.

FRIDAY

SATURDAY

SUNDAY

"**One bad** chapter does not mean your story is over.
So keep going. Write the next chapter.
You've got this." ~ **Rogena Mitchell**

She believed she could so she did.

MONDAY

TUESDAY

WEDNESDAY

THURSDAY

She believed she could so she did.

FRIDAY

SATURDAY

SUNDAY

"**No one** can make you feel inferior without your consent." ~ **Eleanor Roosevelt**

She believed she could so she did.

MONDAY

TUESDAY

WEDNESDAY

THURSDAY

She believed she could so she did.

FRIDAY

SATURDAY

SUNDAY

"The best preparation for tomorrow is
doing your best today." ~ H. Jackson Brown Jr.

She believed she could so she did.

MONDAY

TUESDAY

WEDNESDAY

THURSDAY

She believed she could so she did.

FRIDAY

SATURDAY

SUNDAY

"Start by doing what's necessary; then do what's possible;
and suddenly, you are doing the impossible."
~ Francis of Assisi

She believed she could so she did.

MONDAY

TUESDAY

WEDNESDAY

THURSDAY

She believed she could so she did.

FRIDAY

SATURDAY

SUNDAY

"**How wonderful** it is that nobody need wait a single
moment before starting to improve the world."
~ Anne Frank

She believed she could so she did.

MONDAY

TUESDAY

WEDNESDAY

THURSDAY

She believed she could so she did.

FRIDAY

SATURDAY

SUNDAY

"**Laughter... the** kind that touches every nerve in
your body... starts in the mind, touches the heart, and
reaches the soul." ~ **Rogena Mitchell**

She believed she could so she did.

MONDAY

_____
_____
_____
_____
_____

TUESDAY

_____
_____
_____
_____
_____

WEDNESDAY

_____
_____
_____
_____
_____

THURSDAY

_____
_____
_____

She believed she could so she did.

FRIDAY

SATURDAY

SUNDAY

"**As we** express our gratitude, we must never forget
the highest appreciation is not to utter words but
to live by them." ~ **John F. Kennedy**

She believed she could so she did.

MONDAY

TUESDAY

WEDNESDAY

THURSDAY

She believed she could so she did.

FRIDAY

SATURDAY

SUNDAY

"**Health is** the greatest gift, contentment the greatest wealth, faithfulness the best relationship." ~ **Buddha**

She believed she could so she did.

MONDAY

TUESDAY

WEDNESDAY

THURSDAY

She believed she could so she did.

FRIDAY

_____
_____
_____
_____

SATURDAY

_____
_____
_____
_____
_____

SUNDAY

_____
_____
_____
_____
_____

"**My mission** in life is not merely to survive, but to thrive; and to do so with some passion, some compassion, some humor, and some style." **~ Maya Angelou**

She believed she could so she did.

MONDAY

TUESDAY

WEDNESDAY

THURSDAY

She believed she could so she did.

FRIDAY

SATURDAY

SUNDAY

"No act of kindness, no matter how small,
is ever wasted." – Aesop

She believed she could so she did.

MONDAY

TUESDAY

WEDNESDAY

THURSDAY

She believed she could so she did.

FRIDAY

SATURDAY

SUNDAY

"**If you** believe in yourself and have dedication and pride ~ and never quit, you'll be a winner. The price of victory is high, but so are the rewards." ~ **Paul Bryant**

She believed she could so she did.

MONDAY

TUESDAY

WEDNESDAY

THURSDAY

She believed she could so she did.

FRIDAY

SATURDAY

SUNDAY

"You must do the things you think you
cannot do." ~ Eleanor Roosevelt

She believed she could so she did.

MONDAY

TUESDAY

WEDNESDAY

THURSDAY

She believed she could so she did.

FRIDAY

SATURDAY

SUNDAY

"There are two ways of spreading light: to be the candle
or the mirror that reflects it." ~ Edith Wharton

She believed she could so she did.

MONDAY

TUESDAY

WEDNESDAY

THURSDAY

She believed she could so she did.

FRIDAY

SATURDAY

SUNDAY

"**I believe** in pink. I believe that laughing is the best calorie burner.
I believe in kissing, kissing a lot. I believe in being strong when
everything seems to be going wrong. I believe that happy girls are
the prettiest girls. I believe that tomorrow is another day and
I believe in miracles." ~ **Audrey Hepburn**

She believed she could so she did.

MONDAY

_____
_____
_____
_____

TUESDAY

_____
_____
_____
_____

WEDNESDAY

_____
_____
_____
_____

THURSDAY

_____
_____
_____

She believed she could so she did.

FRIDAY

SATURDAY

SUNDAY

"**A creative** man is motivated by the desire to achieve, not by the desire to beat others." ~ **Ayn Rand**

She believed she could so she did.

MONDAY

TUESDAY

WEDNESDAY

THURSDAY

She believed she could so she did.

FRIDAY

SATURDAY

SUNDAY

"**You will** only find true happiness when you finally stop comparing yourself to other people.
Be You. You are enough." – **Rogena Mitchell**

She believed she could so she did.

MONDAY

TUESDAY

WEDNESDAY

THURSDAY

She believed she could so she did.

FRIDAY

SATURDAY

SUNDAY

"**We can't** help everyone, but everyone can help someone." ~ **Ronald Reagan**

She believed she could so she did.

MONDAY

TUESDAY

WEDNESDAY

THURSDAY

She believed she could so she did.

FRIDAY

SATURDAY

SUNDAY

"**Always do** your best. What you plant now, you will harvest later." ~ **Og Mandino**

She believed she could so she did.

MONDAY

TUESDAY

WEDNESDAY

THURSDAY

She believed she could so she did.

FRIDAY

SATURDAY

SUNDAY

"**What lies** behind you and what lies in front of you,
pales in comparison to what lies
inside of you." ~ **Ralph Waldo Emerson**

She believed she could so she did.

MONDAY

TUESDAY

WEDNESDAY

THURSDAY

She believed she could so she did.

FRIDAY

SATURDAY

SUNDAY

"**The secret** of getting ahead is getting started."
~ Mark Twain

She believed she could so she did.

MONDAY

TUESDAY

WEDNESDAY

THURSDAY

She believed she could so she did.

FRIDAY

SATURDAY

SUNDAY

"**Don't judge** each day by the harvest you reap but by the seeds that you plant." ~ **Robert Louis Stevenson**

She believed she could so she did.

MONDAY

TUESDAY

WEDNESDAY

THURSDAY

She believed she could so she did.

FRIDAY

_____

_____

_____

_____

SATURDAY

_____

_____

_____

_____

SUNDAY

_____

_____

_____

_____

"**In order** to succeed, we must first believe
that we can." ~ **Nikos Kazantzakis**

She believed she could so she did.

MONDAY

TUESDAY

WEDNESDAY

THURSDAY

She believed she could so she did.

FRIDAY

SATURDAY

SUNDAY

"**Start your** day with a smile. Look in the mirror and see
the gleam of the smile in your eyes. Now share the smile,
the gleam, with everyone you meet today."
~ Rogena Mitchell

She believed she could so she did.

MONDAY

TUESDAY

WEDNESDAY

THURSDAY

She believed she could so she did.

FRIDAY

_____

_____

_____

_____

_____

SATURDAY

_____

_____

_____

_____

_____

SUNDAY

_____

_____

_____

_____

_____

"**Let us** remember: One book, one pen, one child, and one teacher can change the world." ~ **Malala Yousafzai**

She believed she could so she did.

MONDAY

TUESDAY

WEDNESDAY

THURSDAY

She believed she could so she did.

FRIDAY

SATURDAY

SUNDAY

"**You are** never too old to set another goal or to dream a new dream." ~ C. S. Lewis

She believed she could so she did.

MONDAY

TUESDAY

WEDNESDAY

THURSDAY

She believed she could so she did.

FRIDAY

SATURDAY

SUNDAY

"Life is 10 percent what you make it and 90 percent how you take it." ~ Irving Berlin

She believed she could so she did.

MONDAY

TUESDAY

WEDNESDAY

THURSDAY

She believed she could so she did.

FRIDAY

SATURDAY

SUNDAY

"**Act like** you expect to get into the end zone."
~ Christopher Morley

She believed she could so she did.

MONDAY

_____
_____
_____
_____
_____

TUESDAY

_____
_____
_____
_____
_____

WEDNESDAY

_____
_____
_____
_____
_____

THURSDAY

_____
_____
_____
_____

She believed she could so she did.

FRIDAY

SATURDAY

SUNDAY

"**When you** have a dream, you've got to grab it and never let go." ~ **Carol Burnett**

She believed she could so she did.

MONDAY

TUESDAY

WEDNESDAY

THURSDAY

She believed she could so she did.

FRIDAY

SATURDAY

SUNDAY

"**Life is** a song ~ sing it. Life is a game ~ play it.
Life is a challenge ~ meet it. Life is a dream ~ realize it.
Life is a sacrifice ~ offer it. Life is love ~ enjoy it."
~ Sai Baba

She believed she could so she did.

MONDAY

TUESDAY

WEDNESDAY

THURSDAY

She believed she could so she did.

FRIDAY

SATURDAY

SUNDAY

"**What if** you gave someone a gift, and they neglected to thank you for it ~ would you be likely to give them another? Life is the same way. In order to attract more of the blessings that life has to offer, you must truly appreciate what you already have." ~ **Ralph Marston**

She believed she could so she did.

MONDAY

TUESDAY

WEDNESDAY

THURSDAY

She believed she could so she did.

FRIDAY

SATURDAY

SUNDAY

"**Courage, my** friends; tis not too late to build a better world." ~ **Tommy Douglas**

She believed she could so she did.

MONDAY

_____

_____

_____

_____

_____

TUESDAY

_____

_____

_____

_____

_____

WEDNESDAY

_____

_____

_____

_____

_____

THURSDAY

_____

_____

_____

_____

She believed she could so she did.

FRIDAY

SATURDAY

SUNDAY

"**Life is** really simple, but we insist on making it complicated." ~ **Confucius**

She believed she could so she did.

MONDAY

TUESDAY

WEDNESDAY

THURSDAY

She believed she could so she did.

FRIDAY

SATURDAY

SUNDAY

"Life isn't about finding yourself. Life is about creating yourself." ~ George Bernard Shaw

She believed she could so she did.

MONDAY

TUESDAY

WEDNESDAY

THURSDAY

She believed she could so she did.

FRIDAY

SATURDAY

SUNDAY

"There is nothing stronger in the world than gentleness."
~ Han Suyin

She believed she could so she did.

MONDAY

TUESDAY

WEDNESDAY

THURSDAY

She believed she could so she did.

FRIDAY

SATURDAY

SUNDAY

"**The person**, be it gentleman or lady, who has not pleasure in a good novel, must be intolerably stupid." ~ **Jane Austen**

She believed she could so she did.

MONDAY

TUESDAY

WEDNESDAY

THURSDAY

She believed she could so she did.

FRIDAY

SATURDAY

SUNDAY

"Be brave enough to live life creatively. The creative place where no one else has ever been." ~ Alan Alda

She believed she could so she did.

MONDAY

TUESDAY

WEDNESDAY

THURSDAY

She believed she could so she did.

FRIDAY

SATURDAY

SUNDAY

"**Find out** who you are and be that person. That's what your soul was put on this Earth to be. Find that truth, live that truth and everything else will come." ~ **Ellen DeGeneres**

She believed she could so she did.

MONDAY

TUESDAY

WEDNESDAY

THURSDAY

She believed she could so she did.

FRIDAY

SATURDAY

SUNDAY

"Most of us have far more courage than we ever dreamed we possessed." ~ Dale Carnegie

She believed she could so she did.

MONDAY

TUESDAY

WEDNESDAY

THURSDAY

She believed she could so she did.

FRIDAY

SATURDAY

SUNDAY

"**The Wright** brothers flew right through the smoke screen of impossibility." ~ **Charles Kettering**

She believed she could so she did.

MONDAY

TUESDAY

WEDNESDAY

THURSDAY

She believed she could so she did.

FRIDAY

_____
_____
_____
_____
_____

SATURDAY

_____
_____
_____
_____
_____

SUNDAY

_____
_____
_____
_____
_____

"**Knowing is** not enough; we must apply.
Willing is not enough; we must do."
~ Johann Wolfgang von Goethe

She believed she could so she did.

MONDAY

TUESDAY

WEDNESDAY

THURSDAY

She believed she could so she did.

FRIDAY

SATURDAY

SUNDAY

"It isn't what we say or think that defines us,
but what we do." ~ Jane Austen

She believed she could so she did.

MONDAY

TUESDAY

WEDNESDAY

THURSDAY

She believed she could so she did.

FRIDAY

SATURDAY

SUNDAY

"**Walking with** a friend in the dark is better than walking alone in the light." ~ **Helen Keller**

She believed she could so she did.

MONDAY

TUESDAY

WEDNESDAY

THURSDAY

She believed she could so she did.

FRIDAY

SATURDAY

SUNDAY

"**I never** considered a difference of opinion in politics,
in religion, in philosophy, as cause for withdrawing
from a friend." ~ **Thomas Jefferson**

She believed she could so she did.

MONDAY

TUESDAY

WEDNESDAY

THURSDAY

She believed she could so she did.

"It is one of the blessings of old friends that you can afford
to be stupid with them." ~ Ralph Waldo Emerson

She believed she could so she did.

MONDAY

TUESDAY

WEDNESDAY

THURSDAY

She believed she could so she did.

FRIDAY

SATURDAY

SUNDAY

"She had a lively, playful disposition that delighted in anything ridiculous." ~ **Jane Austen**

She believed she could so she did.

MONDAY

TUESDAY

WEDNESDAY

THURSDAY

She believed she could so she did.

FRIDAY

SATURDAY

SUNDAY

"**Life is** what happens while you are busy making other plans." ~ **John Lennon**

She believed she could so she did.

MONDAY

_____

TUESDAY

_____

WEDNESDAY

_____

THURSDAY

_____

She believed she could so she did.

FRIDAY

SATURDAY

SUNDAY

"**Beware the** barrenness of a busy life." ~ **Socrates**

She believed she could so she did.

MONDAY

TUESDAY

WEDNESDAY

THURSDAY

She believed she could so she did.

FRIDAY

SATURDAY

SUNDAY

"**How far** you go in life depends on your being tender with the young, compassionate with the aged, sympathetic with the striving and tolerant of the weak and strong.
Because someday in your life you will have been all of these."
~ George Washington Carver

She believed she could so she did.

MONDAY

TUESDAY

WEDNESDAY

THURSDAY

She believed she could so she did.

FRIDAY

SATURDAY

SUNDAY

"**When we** remember we are all mad, the mysteries disappear
and life stands explained." ~ **Mark Twain**

She believed she could so she did.

MONDAY

TUESDAY

WEDNESDAY

THURSDAY

She believed she could so she did.

FRIDAY

SATURDAY

SUNDAY

"**Never be** bullied into silence. Never allow yourself to be made a victim. Accept no one's definition of your life; define yourself." ~ **Harvey Fierstein**

TO ORDER ADDITIONAL JOURNALS, GO TO
AMAZON OR THE CREATESPACE ONLINE STORE.
SEARCH ROGENA MITCHELL-JONES JOURNALS.

OR DIRECT FROM THE AUTHOR AT
ROGENA@ROGENAMITCHELL.COM

ROGENA MITCHELL-JONES MANUSCRIPT SERVICE
WWW.ROGENAMITCHELL.COM

"Having worked as a screenwriter for 31 years, I was worn out by countless battles with clueless development execs who wanted to weigh in on how to 'fix' my screenplays, so I was nervous about hiring an 'editor' to help me refine my first novel. It was my experience that those who could actually write, wrote; those who couldn't write, edited. Rogena changed all that. Frankly, I wouldn't publish a thing without her.

"She was forceful with her criticisms without being intractable. She was collaborative without being pedantic, and most importantly, she took the time to analyze, understand and respect my unique style without trying to impose her own. She's an ace with punctuation, something we ignore in screenwriting, and she's a wiz at formatting, making the "e" in e-book stand for 'easy.'

"I am deeply indebted to her and remain one of her biggest fans. Honestly, if there's anything in my book you don't like, I'd bet real money that it's an instance where I ignored Rogena's advice. That's how good she is."

Kevin Alyn Elders is an Author, Screenwriter, Producer, and Director. From his early works, including the Iron Eagle action adventure series, through his later works, including Echelon Conspiracy, he has sold 23 out of 26 original screenplays and has written in many genres for notable directors, actors and producers such as Oliver Stone, Sean Connery, Sylvester Stallone, Arnold Schwarzenegger, Joel Silver, Albert S. Ruddy, and Louis Gossett Jr. His taut, compelling, suspense-filled narratives have found their latest incarnation in his upcoming Screen Novel Series of Paperbacks, EBooks, and Audiobooks. www.kevinalynelders.com.

* * * * *

"On the shore, there was a voice of reason. It was a voice who spoke of telling a story, not about gerunds and gerundives. It spoke of the power of words strung together, not only to convey a concept, but also to tell a story, to draw forth from the reader their untold, unrealized story. And the voice was Rogena Mitchell-Jones."

Baer Charlton, Author of the Pulitzer Prize Nominated book, STONEHEART: A Path of Identity and Redemption

Rogena Mitchell-Jones Manuscript Service

A Professional Editing Service | Freelance Editing with Affordable Rates
Striving for Excellence for You, the Author, Providing Concise Literary & Technical Editing.

"MY NAME IS ROGENA, AND I AM A BOOKAHOLIC."

THE FIRST STEP IS ADMISSION, RIGHT? OK, SERIOUSLY.

Currently, Rogena Mitchell-Jones lives in South Jersey with her wife, Karen, and their extremely pampered cats. If she isn't at home editing or reading, you might find her on the beach—book in hand.

Her background consists of over 25 years in journalism and now editing full time for independent authors internationally since 2013. Her clientele base includes a vast array of Amazon, USA Today, and NY Times Best Selling Authors.

The end of 2014, Rogena was nominated as best editor in an awards event sponsored by The Kindle Hub—TKH Book Awards 2014. With nearly sixty editors competing, she advanced to the finals and came in second in the final competition. With the title of BEST EDITOR 2014 Finalist, it shows hard work does pay off.

She isn't a writer—She's an editor. She is here because she wants to assist you, the author, in creating a manuscript free of typographical errors, including misspelled words, grammatical errors, and inconsistencies in plot and characters.

She gives attention to detail. With this attention to detail, she is able to polish your future best seller, like polishing fine silver that once belonged to your grandmother. Let's make your manuscript the masterpiece you have dreamed of publishing.

She is an editor, not an author. She is a reader, not a writer. She is a Copy Editor. She wants to live in your story while reading your manuscript.

She is here to assist you so you will have a result allowing your future readers to enjoy your published work.

Contact her on Facebook or via email at rogena@rogenamitchell.com.

ROGENA MITCHELL-JONES MANUSCRIPT SERVICE
WWW.ROGENAMITCHELL.COM

CPSIA information can be obtained
at www.ICGtesting.com
Printed in the USA
LVHW101038270219
608900LV00017B/308/P